The Golden Anniversaries

# The Golden Anniversaries

Mark Crawford

*The Golden Anniversaries*
first published 2025 by Scirocco Drama
An imprint of J. Gordon Shillingford Publishing Inc.
© 2025 Mark Crawford

Scirocco Drama Editor: Glenda MacFarlane
Cover design by Doowah Design
Author photo by Ann Baggley Photography
Production photos by Gemma James-Smith and Lyon Smith

Printed and bound in Canada on 100% post-consumer recycled paper.



**Production inquiries to:**
Colin Rivers, Marquis Literary
10 Adelaide Street East, Suite 402
Toronto, Ontario M5C 1J3
416-960-9123 x 223
info@mqlit.ca


*Library and Archives Canada Cataloguing in Publication*

Title: The golden anniversaries / Mark Crawford.
Names: Crawford, Mark, 1981- author.
Identifiers: Canadiana 20250181827 | ISBN 9781990738692 (softcover)
Subjects: LCGFT: Drama.
Classification: LCC PS8605.R435 G65 2025 | DDC C812/.6—dc23


J.Gordon Shillingford Publishing respectfully acknowledges that we are located in Winnipeg, which is on Treaty 1 territory, the traditional lands of the Anishinaabe, Cree, Oji-Cree, Dene, and Dakota Peoples, and the homeland of the Métis Nation.

We acknowledge the financial support of the Canada Council for the Arts, the Government of Canada, the Manitoba Arts Council, and the Manitoba Government for our publishing program.

J. Gordon Shillingford Publishing
P.O. Box 86, RPO Corydon Avenue, Winnipeg, MB Canada R3M 3S3

*For Miles Potter: director, dramaturge, friend.*

*Thanks for everything, buddy.*

# Mark Crawford

Mark Crawford is one of Canada's most popular playwrights. His work has been produced across the country and internationally. He is the author of *Stag and Doe; Bed and Breakfast; The Birds and the Bees; Boys, Girls, and Other Mythological Creatures; The New Canadian Curling Club; Chase the Ace; The Gig;* and *The Golden Anniversaries.* Several of these titles are published by Scirocco Drama. Mark has been longlisted for the Stephen Leacock Medal for Humour and nominated for the Playwrights' Guild of Canada Comedy Award. Also an actor, he has performed at theatres from coast to coast. Mark grew up on his family's farm near Glencoe, Ontario, studied at the University of Toronto and Sheridan College, and now lives in Stratford.

www.markcrawfordplays.com

# Acknowledgements

The playwright acknowledges the artists involved in the premiere production for their work on the development of this play. Special thanks to the Blyth Festival Theatre: Gil Garratt, Artistic Director, Severn Thompson, Associate Artistic Director, and Rachael King, General Manager.

# Foreword

In my capacity as the Artistic Director of the Blyth Festival I've welcomed thousands of people through to the doors, to take their seats (turn off their phones…people please…just turn off your phones), and sit back as we dim the lights and reel them into the world as drawn by Mark Crawford.

That world as drawn by Mark Crawford is one that you instantly recognize. It's as familiar to you as your old neighbourhood, your hometown, your last apartment. It's a place you know. A place of comfort and trust. Mark is the kind of writer who makes sure that you have a comfortable seat, a refreshed drink, a deep breath…. And then he starts to slowly, and with hilarious precision, pull the rug out from under you. You laugh the whole time he's tugging it. But once it goes, once it's gone, you realize that just like your old hometown, everything has changed, and so have you.

I've had the privilege of seeing several of Mark's shows from page to stage. *Stag and Doe*, *The Birds and the Bees*, *The New Canadian Curling Club*, to name a few. In each instance, I had the chance to see these plays as sketches of scenes on a page, beside notes that said, "Insert more dialogue here," "She should make a choice here," "Is this enough of a reason?"…often beside Mark's hand-drawn circles and arrows…the scribbles and marginalia that capture the impulses of a playwright who can already see the play.

Sitting in a roomful of engaged, laughing people on opening night, when one of these shows takes to the boards, is invigorating and entertaining, and always inspiring. Inspiring because at their core, I know that while that audience is rapt in the joyful music, I have seen the conductor's notes…it's all according to plan.

With *The Golden Anniversaries*, I experienced an even more rare privilege: before Mark had even written a word of the play, he sent me a note that said: "I want to write a play that will make my father cry."

Well…that sure got my attention.

Why would someone want to write a play that makes their father cry? Revenge? Rebellion? Just to be a little jerk…? Nope. Release.

"To let him feel something. Feel something real. To set myself the task of writing something deep and meaningful enough that it leaks out of my dad's eyes."

It's rare to be trusted by an artist to this degree…to have them reveal the very first flicker of their new fire.

What Mark set off to do with *The Golden Anniversaries* was to write a play that was both hysterically funny and deeply dismantling. Here he has captured a portrait of Long Term Love, of a full Love Life, a full Life full of Love, that finds itself woven with the filaments of intimacy that weave a couple's life together, forever.

This is a simple play, but not a simplistic play.

Not a lighthearted play, but a play whose heart is full of light.

Mark has done that thing we so often aspire to onstage: taken the strongest most dependable thing that we lean on, and shown us just how fragile it can actually be.

I was comfortable in my chair. My drink was refreshed. I sat back and laughed my head off. Mark pulled the rug out. And in that moment, I saw what was holding up the floor. And it changed me.

Gil Garratt

*Gil Garratt is a director, playwright, and actor. He is the Artistic Director of the Blyth Festival.*

# Production History

*The Golden Anniversaries* was commissioned and developed by the Blyth Festival Theatre.

The world première was produced by the Blyth Festival in July of 2024, with the following cast and creative team:

Glen .................................................................. Jim Mezon

Sandy .................................................. Janet-Laine Green

Director ......................................................... Miles Potter

Stage Manager ............................................... Ann Stuart

Assistant Stage Manager ............ Amanda McDonnell

Set Designer ................................................. Steve Lucas

Lighting Designer ..................................... Nic Vincent

Costume Designer .................................. Amanda Wong

Sound Designer ............................................ Lyon Smith

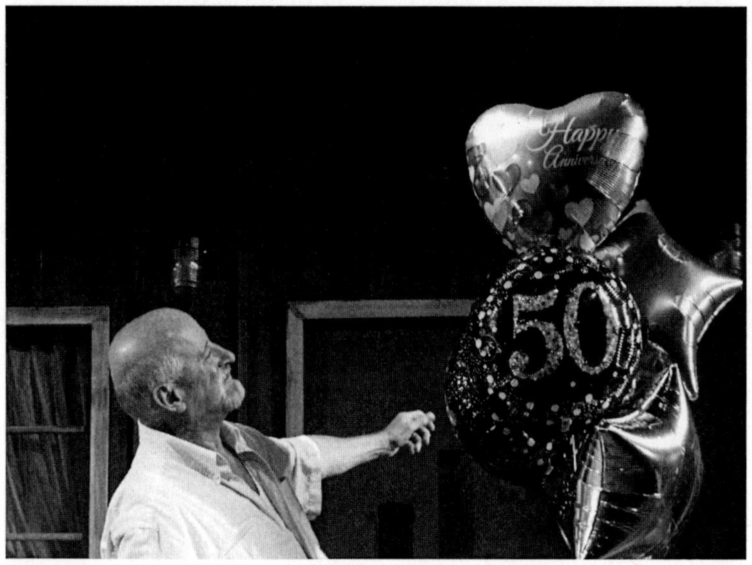

Glen admires the balloons in anticipation of Sandy's arrival. Photo of Jim Mezon by Gemma James-Smith.

Glen and Sandy on their wedding night. Photo of Jim Mezon and Janet-Laine Green by Gemma James-Smith.

The silver anniversary necklace. Photo of Jim Mezon and Janet-Laine Green by Gemma James-Smith.

Sandy holds up The Golden's sign. Photo of Janet-Laine Green by Gemma James-Smith.

Glen and Sandy's 30th anniversary. Photo of Jim Mezon and Janet-Laine Green by Gemma James-Smith.

The Goldens' 44th anniversary. Photo of Janet-Laine Green and Jim Mezon by Lyon Smith.

Glen comforts Sandy in the present. Photo of Jim Mezon and Janet-Laine Green by Gemma James-Smith.

Glen and Sandy look at the stars. Photo of Jim Mezon and Janet-Laine Green by Gemma James-Smith.

# Characters

GLEN

SANDY

*Both are in their early seventies. We also see them at various ages over the past fifty years.*

# Setting

The deck of a cottage on the lake. The cottage itself was likely built in the 1930s or '40s—one of thousands of single-storey two-bedroom structures that line the shores of lakes all over the country. There's nothing fancy about it, but it's not rundown. The overall feel is that of a cozy family cottage.

There are steps on either side of the deck, leading to the ground on each side of the cottage. There are also large steps across the front. At centre, there is a door to the cottage, and on the exterior walls, a few windows. We can glimpse the interior of the cottage through the windows at certain times of day.

On the deck is an outdoor table and two chairs, and a few other places to perch—benches or low railings or other outdoor furniture. There are a couple of potted plants—some thriving, some not; a rain gauge containing a few inches of water; an outdoor lantern with a candle inside; and a barbecue off to one side.

It's an evening in late July in the present—and this same date for the past fifty years.

As the play begins, it's around 7:00pm. Throughout the scenes in the present, the sun goes down so that by the final scene, it's dark. The memory scenes happen at various times of day.

# Notes on Production

*Memory Scenes*

When moving between the present and the past, there should be no big break in the action. The lights change to indicate a different time of day, or different weather, and these transitions into and out of memory should be supported by sound. Sometimes, these memories can take a few seconds to establish. Other times, the switch in time is almost instant. Most importantly, there are no costume changes or attempts to make Glen and Sandy appear younger. That's all done through the power of acting.

*Wardrobe*

The clothes that Sandy and Glen are wearing should be appropriate for this evening in the present, but neutral enough to also work for scenes in the past. For example, in Act One, Sandy is dressed to go out for dinner in the present, but this must double as her going-away outfit on her wedding night, what she's wearing during a heat wave, and to a nice restaurant for their 25th anniversary. For both characters for both acts, I suggest fairly neutral colours and clean lines.

*Sound and Music*

For the top-of-show music, it's fun to use a popular song from 50 years ago. Sandy's reference to the band or singer on page 22 can change depending on the song choice. Please consult with the playwright to change this line accordingly.

For the transitions into and out of memory, this is open to interpretation. I suggest creating sounds with a sense of movement—as though we're being drawn back and forth in time. You might want to incorporate some of the ambient sounds of the outdoors at the cottage, or something that says, "memory" to you.

*Running Time*

Act One runs approximately 52 minutes and Act Two approximately 32 minutes.

## Act One

*The top-of-show music plays—a recognizable, upbeat song from 50 years ago. In the original production, it was "Ain't Seen Nothing Yet" by Bachman-Turner Overdrive. The sound transitions from the theatre speakers to a small portable stereo, which is being carried from inside the cottage onto the deck by GLEN. He's also holding a bottle of wine. GLEN hums and dances along to the tune. He sets the stereo down to one side and places the wine on the table. He goes back inside and comes out a moment later with a bunch of helium balloons that say "50" and "Happy Anniversary." He places them on the table. Then, he gets bitten by a mosquito…and another. He pops his head inside and grabs a can of bug spray. He applies it to his exposed skin; at first, a normal amount—but then he absolutely douses himself. Now, in addition to the music, we hear a car pull up and park behind the cottage. This gets GLEN's attention. The car door closes. GLEN stashes the bug spray inside, checks that everything is ready, and goes to the SL steps to watch his visitor arrive, taking a deep breath to calm himself. SANDY hurries on from the SR side—unbeknownst to GLEN. She takes in the scene, then flicks off the stereo. GLEN turns around, startled to see her there.*

GLEN:        AH! Oh my God. What are you trying to do, kill me?

SANDY:       The thought has crossed my mind. So. What's wrong?

GLEN:        What do you mean?

SANDY:       You said there's an emergency.

GLEN:        I did?

SANDY:       Yes. In your text.

*GLEN gets out his phone and looks.*

So, what's the matter?

GLEN:        *(Reading the text.)* I said, "Come to the cottage."

SANDY:       *(Snatching his phone.)* No, you said, *(Reading.)* "Sandy: I need you to come to the cottage immediately."

GLEN:        Okay…

SANDY:       There's a difference, Glen.

GLEN:        Right.

SANDY:       *(Still reading.)* I said: "What's going on?" and you said, "Just get here." Then I said, "Is everything okay?" and you said: "No."

GLEN:        *(Taking his phone back.)* I never said emergency.

SANDY:       Glen! I drove here like a bat out of hell. I thought the cottage was on fire. I thought I was going to find you dead.

GLEN:        Well…no such luck.

SANDY:       Oh my God.

GLEN:       I didn't mean to cause alarm.

SANDY:      Well, you did.

GLEN:       *(Looking at the texts.)* I guess I can see how you might have got a bit confused.

SANDY:      I'm not confused.

GLEN:       It doesn't matter. What matters is you're here now.

SANDY:      What is all this? *(The wine, balloons, etc.)*

GLEN:       Well…it's today.

SANDY:      I know what day it is, Glen, why are there balloons?

GLEN:       Aren't they great? I was picking up some things in town and they have a counter with party supplies in the back of Canadian Tire now, and I thought, "If I don't get these, who will?"

SANDY:      Oh, I don't know: couples who are still together!?

GLEN:       Sandy, c'mon. Fifty years? I figured we could—

SANDY:      What? Celebrate? You are unbelievable, you know that? I got here in record time, under an hour, because I thought something was wrong.

GLEN:       Something *was* wrong. Not seeing you— today of all days—it felt wrong.

SANDY:      Well, here I am. You've seen me. I've seen you. Happy What-Would-Have-Been-Our-50th-Anniversary. *(She starts to go.)*

GLEN:       You're not leaving.

SANDY:    (*Stopping.*) I am. What, you think I'm going to stick around for Bachman-Turner Overbite and a bunch of balloons?

GLEN:    Honey, we need to talk.

SANDY:    Talk! No, I see what you're trying to do here. You're trying to wine and dine me and win me back.

GLEN:    That's not what I'm— I'd like to have a conversation. About what's going on.

SANDY:    What's going on is, I finally had enough of your bullshit and said, "Pack your bags and get out." How's that for a conversation?

GLEN:    That is not what I'm talking about and you know it.

SANDY:    Glen.

GLEN:    We need to discuss it. Like reasonable people. But we can't do that if you never answer my calls, don't reply to my texts—

SANDY:    I just did.

GLEN:    The other night when I tried to come home, you wouldn't let me through the door—of my own house.

SANDY:    Because I kicked you out. What part of that don't you understand?

GLEN:    I thought it was just for a night or two—cool down, clear our heads—but it's been over a week now. I had to go to Walmart and buy new underwear.

SANDY:    You bought your own underwear? Well! Miracles do happen.

GLEN:    So is this your plan? Shut me out? Pretend I don't exist? You don't want to talk? Fine. I can't make you. But it is still our anniversary: even if we called off the party, even if we're not living under the same roof, that doesn't change the fact that we have spent the last half century together. You don't want balloons? Fine. Here. No balloons. *(He picks them up.)* But fifty years, Sandy. You can't just throw me away.

*He takes the balloons inside. SANDY sets down her purse.*

SANDY:    They sell balloons at Canadian Tire? God, they really do have everything.

*SANDY crosses to the table. Just as her hand reaches for the wine bottle, GLEN re-enters.*

GLEN:    You want some of that?

SANDY:    Nope.

GLEN:    They didn't have that kind in town.

SANDY:    What?

GLEN:    I had to go to the big liquor store.

SANDY:    Oh.

GLEN.    *(Showing her the label.)* That's the one, right? Your favourite?

SANDY:    Yeah.

GLEN:    Well, let's crack it open.

SANDY:    No, I'm driving back.

GLEN:    You just got here.

SANDY:        I'm fine.

GLEN:         (*A move towards the door.*) I'll grab the glasses.

SANDY:        I said I'm fine.

GLEN:         If we're going to sit and talk, we can at least have a glass of wine.

SANDY:        Glen?

GLEN:         I got it for you.

SANDY:        (*Firmly.*) Glen.

>            *He puts the wine down.*

>            Thank you.

>            *Beat.*

GLEN:         Why'd you come down that way?

SANDY:        What?

GLEN:         I was watching for you here, but you came around the side. We never go that way.

SANDY:        Oh. Um— (*She points to the way he was looking, SR.*)

GLEN:         Ohhh, is it that downspout? (*He looks.*) Ah, yeah. It's all muddy. I didn't even think of that.

SANDY:        Muddy? It's like a landslide over there. I didn't want to slip.

GLEN:         Did it rain at home?

SANDY:        What, when?

GLEN:         This afternoon.

SANDY:        ...No.

GLEN:   *(Picking up the full rain gauge.)* No? It poured here.

SANDY:   Okay.

GLEN:   Would you look at that?

SANDY:   Uh huh.

GLEN:   A monsoon!

> *He pours the water into a dead-looking potted plant.*

SANDY:   Have you lost weight?

GLEN:   What?

SANDY:   I think you've lost weight.

GLEN:   Since when? I was at home?

SANDY:   Turn around. *(He hesitates.)* Turn. *(He does.)* You have. Your ass is gone.

GLEN:   *(Tries to see his ass.)* What?

SANDY:   It's the first thing to go—anytime you lose a few pounds. You used to have such a cute little ass, but look at it now. Flat. As a pancake. Have you been eating?

GLEN:   Yes.

SANDY:   Where? The diner?

GLEN:   No. Some. But I've been making most of my own meals.

SANDY:   Man cannot live on wieners and beans alone.

GLEN:   I got other stuff.

SANDY:   Yeah? Like what?

GLEN:          …I didn't do a big shop cuz I didn't know how long I'd be here.

SANDY:         Well, feel free to stock up.

GLEN:          I've been exercising. That's probably why I look so fit.

SANDY:         Exercising?

GLEN:          Yeah, Stacey showed me a thing on my phone that tracks my steps. I've been walking. Ten thousand steps, every day. You have any idea how far that is?

SANDY:         About ten thousand steps?

GLEN:          Exactly. And in the mornings, I've been uh, going to *(Mumbles.)* yoga.

SANDY:         What was that?

GLEN:          Yoga. I'm doing yoga.

SANDY:         You?

GLEN:          Greg said it might help with my, uh… *(Does a gesture for his mind.)* There's a seniors' class in town. I've been three times now. I know all the moves: Mountain. Pigeon. …Shavasana.

SANDY:         Well! Namaste. So you've talked to them then.

GLEN:          Who?

SANDY:         The kids.

GLEN:          Of course. Everyone came up on the weekend.

SANDY:         Oh.

GLEN:          Well, Tim had a golf tournament, so he came late. But Greg and Nicky, Stacey—

SANDY:      And the girls?

GLEN:       …I left you three voicemails asking if you wanted to come.

SANDY:      The kids don't want to see me. They've made that perfectly clear.

GLEN:       Greg told me he's been over to the house every day.

SANDY:      Stacey, I mean.

GLEN:       She's…upset.

SANDY:      Oh, cuz I made her cancel the big anniversary party? Well, I'm sorry she can't get her money back for the cake.

GLEN:       That's not why she's upset and you know it.

SANDY:      What did her email say?

GLEN:       What?

SANDY:      Her email telling everyone the party was off. I ran into…oh, the lady down the street—

GLEN:       Who?

SANDY:      Our neighbour.

GLEN:       Parvati?

SANDY:      Parvati? No. You know, the lady. On the corner. They were invited?

GLEN:       Suzanne?

SANDY:      Suzanne! God. Me and names.

GLEN:       Yeah… What about her?

SANDY:    She was in a big tizzy. "Sandy! I got your daughter's email. You're not having your 50th? Is everything okay?" I said, "Everything's fine, Suzanne. Nothing to worry about. We decided not to have the party cuz I kicked Glen to the curb."

GLEN:    Nice.

SANDY:    Then she says, "After fifty years? Oh, Sandy! But why?"

GLEN:    And what'd you tell her?

SANDY:    "Because, Suzanne: he drove me up the fucking wall."

GLEN:    *(He laughs.)* Did that shut her up?

SANDY:    For once. *(Quick beat.)* You know, I cannot believe you managed to drag me here again.

GLEN:    Drag you here?

SANDY:    The exact same place, the exact same day.

GLEN:    You always loved it.

SANDY:    But every single year? For fifty years?

GLEN:    It's our thing.

SANDY:    Whatever.

GLEN:    No, not "whatever." It's pretty amazing, if you ask me: the fact that we always made time for it; that we never missed a year. I think that's something.

SANDY:    Oh, it's something all right.

GLEN:    Most couples don't have an anniversary tradition like this.

SANDY:    No, most couples just go for a nice dinner and then think about having sex.

GLEN:    But don't.

SANDY:    And most couples don't have this anniversary tradition because most couples didn't wind up at a random cottage on their wedding night by mistake.

GLEN:    Yeah, but just imagine if they hadn't screwed up our reservation, we never would have come here in the first place.

SANDY:    If who hadn't screwed up?

GLEN:    The people at the Inn.

SANDY:    No, you screwed up, Glen. That's why we had to stay here.

GLEN:    What? No.

SANDY:    Yes. It was my wedding night, I think I remember.

GLEN:    It was my wedding night too.

SANDY:    Yeah, and you were half-cut.

GLEN:    Was not.

SANDY:    You had a drink before you even got to the altar.

GLEN:    For courage. Cuz I was marrying you. I'm sorry, dear, but you're remembering it wrong.

SANDY:    I remember like it was yesterday. We left our wedding reception, I drove us to the Inn—

GLEN:    Someone screwed up our reservation—

SANDY:      You. So we came here. And I...really had to pee...

            ***Transition to fifty years ago. GLEN and SANDY's wedding night.***

            *It's late at night, and dark on the deck. GLEN fumbles with a ring of keys. He is drunk and SANDY's gotta go.*

GLEN:       Okay, okay, okay.

SANDY:      I gotta go.

GLEN:       Yeah, yeah, yeah, just gimme a sec.

SANDY:      *(Holding it.)* Ughh...

GLEN:       *(Searching through the keys.)* It's not my fault they gave away our room.

SANDY:      I know.

GLEN:       I called weeks ago; told them to book the best room they got—

SANDY:      He said it's a square key.

GLEN:       But nooo, "Sorry, young man, there's nothing under that name."

SANDY:      Square.

GLEN:       "We're fully booked. No vacancy!"

SANDY:      Glen...

GLEN:       You just used the washroom at the Inn.

SANDY:      I know, I have to go again.

GLEN:       You weren't even drinking tonight.

SANDY:      You had enough for both of us.

GLEN:    I'm not even drunk! *(With a gesture, the keys fly out of his hand.)* Aw, crap. *(Picks them up.)* Then he goes, "Did you write down your reservation, young man?" and I go, yeah, here, cuz I had it on a piece of paper, right? But I musta left it in my suit.

SANDY:    I know.

GLEN:    So I go, "It's my wedding night, man. That's my wife in the can." Ha! You're my wife!

SANDY:    Okay, can I try?

GLEN:    I got it. *(Moving towards the door.)* But nope! No room at the Inn! We're like Mary and Joseph.

SANDY:    *(Uncomfortable.)* Uh huh.

GLEN:    Think there's gonna be a manger inside? Ox and lamb?

SANDY:    As long as there's a washroom, I don't give a shit.

GLEN:    Hey, hey, hey! Language. Are you mad at me?

SANDY:    I just really have to pee!

GLEN:    *(A new key.)* Ah, here we go!

SANDY:    Thank God.

GLEN:    *(It doesn't work.)* Oh, nope.

SANDY:    Uggggghhhh!

GLEN:    If it's that bad, go in the bushes.

SANDY:    I am not going in the bushes, Glen.

GLEN:    I'll come with you.

SANDY:    No!

GLEN:        To protect you!

SANDY:       Do you know where my sister went on her honeymoon?

GLEN:        (*Sheepish.*) Paris.

SANDY:       Paris. France. And we were going to a little inn on the lake.

GLEN:        Well, sorry I'm not made of money like Richard.

SANDY:       No, I was happy with our plan; I was excited; but clearly something happened with our reservation—

GLEN:        They lost it!

SANDY:       And if it weren't for that nice old man behind the desk giving us the keys to his own cottage, we'd be shit out of luck—

GLEN:        It's the least he could do.

SANDY:       So I do not need to go to Paris, but it is still my wedding night, and I draw the line at squatting in the bush. So open the goddamn door!

               *GLEN tries another key. It doesn't work.*

             Move.

               *She tries it.*

GLEN:        He gave us the wrong keys.

SANDY:       Oh, come on…

GLEN:        (*Turning to go.*) I'll go ask him.

SANDY:       You stupid piece of shit.

GLEN:        (*Turning back.*) Hey!

SANDY:    The door. (*Trying one more key.*) Open up, you sonofabitch, I gotta GO!

*And the door opens. She runs inside.*

GLEN:    Well. You told him.

*A light turns on inside, and an interior door closes. GLEN pops his head in and flicks on the outdoor light. He stays outside to have a smoke. He gets a cigarette out, lights up, and hums to himself—a love song from around the time they were married. He spots the candle in the lantern, and lights it up too. His humming turns to singing and he slow dances with an invisible partner. He dips her and...*

**Transition back to the present day— GLEN and SANDY's 50th anniversary.** *SANDY re-enters. GLEN palms his cigarette, the candle goes out, and the lights return to early evening. They are standing where they were when the memory began.*

GLEN:    Whoa, whoa, whoa, whoa, whoa.

SANDY:    What?

GLEN:    I did not sing that song.

SANDY:    You did so.

GLEN:    No, you are making that part up.

SANDY:    I heard you, Glen.

GLEN:    No.

SANDY:    Through the bathroom window.

GLEN:    That song?

SANDY:          It was our first dance. I heard you singing it out here.

GLEN:           And you remember that?

SANDY:          Steel trap. *(Her brain.)*

GLEN:           Well, you still haven't proved I screwed up the reservation.

SANDY:          I'm getting there. If you don't interrupt.

> *GLEN gestures for her to continue and mumbles, "Oh, well, please…"*

So. I come back from the bathroom…

> *Transition back to the past: 50 years ago. SANDY has just closed the door, coming back from the bathroom. GLEN is smoking, the candle is burning. Still the middle of the night, but the outdoor light is on.*

GLEN:           How is it in there?

SANDY:          Not bad, actually.

GLEN:           It's no Paris.

SANDY:          Oh, forget Paris. Debra didn't even have a good time. She told me Richard spent the whole trip complaining that everyone spoke French. He may have money, but he don't have class.

GLEN:           Your parents sure love him.

SANDY:          They love you too.

> *GLEN's not buying it. He puts out his cigarette.*

They do! They're just…uptight.

GLEN:    Your mom was cutting a rug on the dance floor.

SANDY:    Until my dad told her to stop. Oh God, I don't want to turn into them.

GLEN:    We won't. At least both of your folks were there.

SANDY:    Yeah.

GLEN:    It's fine. It's good my dad didn't come. That would have been a train wreck.

SANDY:    Your mom seemed to be in good spirits today.

GLEN:    She can put on a show when she needs to. Oh, but my brother!

SANDY:    Oh my God.

GLEN:    I mean, Bill, buddy, it's one thing to leave your pregnant wife for another woman. It's a whole other thing to bring your new gal to my wedding.

SANDY:    Wearing that dress.

GLEN:    If you can call it a dress. Centrefolds wear more clothes than that. So I've heard.

SANDY:    She seems like a sweet girl. Cheryl?

GLEN:    Sharon.

SANDY:    Sharon.

GLEN:    When she walked into the church, all the men's heads turned. I thought your Uncle Marty was gonna pass out. And the minister. A-wooga!

*GLEN laughs. SANDY's mood shifts.*

It was a great day.

SANDY:      I know. I just uh… There's something I have
            to tell you.

GLEN:       Okay…

SANDY:      But you have to promise me you'll keep your
            cool.

GLEN:       What is it?

SANDY:      Promise?

GLEN:       Tell me first and then I'll decide.

SANDY:      I didn't say anything earlier because I didn't
            want to ruin the day.

GLEN:       Say what?

SANDY:      Oh my God. I can't believe this is happening.

GLEN:       Sandy…

SANDY:      We had this whole life plan, and now
            everything's out the window.

GLEN:       What?

SANDY:      I'm supposed to start teaching in September,
            but I don't even know if I should—

GLEN:       Sandy! What are you talking about?

SANDY:      I'm… We…are going to have a baby.

GLEN:       …What?

SANDY:      Don't freak out.

GLEN:       No…what?

SANDY:      I thought it was a false alarm, so I didn't say
            anything, but I went to the doctor, and he
            called me last night—

GLEN:        I thought you were saying we made a mistake.

SANDY:       We did.

GLEN:        No, getting married.

SANDY:       What? No.

GLEN:        But wait, wait, wait, wait, wait, how can this be? You're on the pill.

SANDY:       Yeah, and I was also on antibiotics?

GLEN:        We were careful.

SANDY:       Except that one time…

GLEN:        I pulled out!

SANDY:       But then you…you know…

GLEN:        …Oh my God. They really *can* swim.

SANDY:       Did we have a shotgun wedding?

GLEN:        What?

SANDY:       No, this isn't the reason we got married.

GLEN:        You just found out.

SANDY:       But people will do the math.

GLEN:        Who?

SANDY:       My parents, they'll count backwards, they'll know.

GLEN:        So?

SANDY:       So: things are supposed to happen in a certain order. I wanted us to have time to enjoy being married first.

GLEN:        We will.

SANDY:       I wanted to work on my writing. That was the plan: teach for a few years, write a book in my spare time, get published—

GLEN:        You still can do that.

SANDY:       And you. You don't want to work for Bill forever.

GLEN:        It's not so bad.

SANDY:       Glen, you hate it.

GLEN:        Yeah, well, people need cars.

SANDY:       You can do something else, you know.

GLEN:        It's fine. I'll provide for us—our family. You don't have to work.

SANDY:       I want to.

GLEN:        And by Thanksgiving, it'll be: *(His high school boy.)* "Hey Mrs. Golden, are you knocked up?"

SANDY:       *(Pained.)* Mrs. Golden.

GLEN:        Easier than Miss Wasikowska.

SANDY:       Still sounds like a paint colour. "We're redoing the living room and can't decide: Dusty Caramel or Sandy Golden?"

GLEN:        What should we name this one?

SANDY:       Oh God, we have to give it a name?

GLEN:        Do you think it's a boy or a girl?

SANDY:       Probably.

GLEN:         The Golden Child! Things may be a bit out of order, but…are you excited?

SANDY:        Yes. And scared.

GLEN:         I'm not going anywhere. I'm not like Bill.

SANDY:        I know.

GLEN:         Or my dad. You don't wanna turn into your folks, I don't wanna turn into them.

SANDY:        Let's not turn into Debra and Richard either.

GLEN:         Oh, God, no! We are going to do it right. We are going to be happy.

              *SANDY gives him a kiss. Then she gets frisky and goes to undo his belt.*

              Hey, hey, hey!

SANDY:        Hey what?

GLEN:         Did you want to… Now?

SANDY:        It's still our wedding night.

GLEN:         But the baby. What if I poke it?

SANDY:        It's the size of a pea, Glen. Don't flatter yourself.

              *They get back to it. SANDY puts her hands in his back pockets to pull him close. She finds a piece of paper in there and pulls it out.*

              Hey! You didn't leave it in your suit.

GLEN:         What? (*Snatches it and looks.*) Ah! Let's go back to the Inn, we can show him this—

SANDY:        (*Takes it back.*) Wait.

GLEN:        Now we're really like Mary and Joseph—

SANDY:       Honey?

GLEN:        He has to give us a room.

SANDY:       This is the wrong inn.

GLEN:        *(Taking the paper back.)* What?

SANDY:       You made a reservation somewhere else.

GLEN:        No.

SANDY:       Yes.

GLEN:        Idiot!

SANDY:       Hey! We don't need no stinkin' inn. *(She rips up the paper and hands it back to him. She looks around.)* I like it here. *(She looks out.)* Look! You can see the stars!

> GLEN *looks out as well.* SANDY *reaches over and takes hold of his hand.*
>
> **Transition back to the present.** *The candle and outdoor light go out, and the lights return to the evening of their 50th anniversary.* GLEN *and* SANDY *let go of each other's hands. She takes a step away.*

GLEN:        Huh.

SANDY:       You remember now? You made the mistake.

GLEN:        Maybe it wasn't a mistake, though. Maybe it was…divine intervention.

SANDY:       Divine intervention?

GLEN:        Yeah. Like, this place was destined to be part of our life.

SANDY:          Oh my God, man, just admit you screwed up.

GLEN:           Fine. I screwed up. Happy now?

SANDY:          Delighted. Only took you fifty years. (*Quick beat.*) What is that smell?

GLEN:           What smell?

SANDY:          Is that you?

GLEN:           Oh. Bug spray.

SANDY:          How much did you put on?

GLEN:           Not much.

SANDY:          Seriously?

GLEN:           Have you seen the mosquitoes this year? After a rain like that, they're enormous. The size of hummingbirds. One landed on me yesterday, I watched its whole body fill up with blood.

SANDY:          Did you pass out?

GLEN:           No. I practised my breathing. (*He demonstrates briefly: in and out through his nose, standing in yoga mountain pose.*) You want some?

SANDY:          Bug spray? No, they never bother me.

GLEN:           Yeah, they don't care for cold blood.

SANDY:          Well, this has been fun. (*She heads for her purse.*)

GLEN:           Kidding! I'm kidding.

                         *She stops.*

                Why are you all dressed up?

SANDY:          What?

GLEN:           You just…you look nice.

SANDY:          Oh.

GLEN:           Haven't lost your ass.

*She shoots him a look.*

That's a good thing! It's a great ass. Don't lose it. I just wondered if you were going out.

SANDY:          …Oh, shit! *(She gets her phone out of her purse.)*

GLEN:           What?

SANDY:          I'm supposed to be having dinner.

GLEN:           Where?

SANDY:          Back home.

GLEN:           Was someone coming over?

SANDY:          No, at a restaurant. But then you sent that stupid text—

GLEN:           Who were you having dinner with?

SANDY:          *(Reading a text.)* Jesus H. Christ.

GLEN:           Oh. Well, say hi to him for me.

SANDY:          What?

GLEN:           Nothing.

SANDY:          Oh, great! He's eating without me.

GLEN:           What, are you going to go?

SANDY:          *(Texting a reply.)* No, by the time I get back, he'll be gone—

GLEN:           Who is it?

SANDY:      Never mind. God, Glen, I was all ready to go, but then you distracted me and now… Shit.

*She puts her phone away.*

GLEN:       Do you want something to eat? I can make us dinner.

SANDY:      Wieners and beans? I'll pass.

*She moves her purse to the side.*

GLEN:       Oh! I didn't tell you who I met at the visitation.

SANDY:      Whose visitation?

GLEN:       Pat's.

SANDY:      What, like Patty?

GLEN:       No, not Patty. Patty's fine. She was out on her deck after the rain. *(The next cottage over.)* Patrick. Hargrave, you know, from the Inn. Who gave us the keys that night? Pat!

SANDY:      He *just* died?

GLEN:       Well, last Thursday.

SANDY:      How old was he?

GLEN:       A hundred and four.

SANDY:      Oh my God. He seemed old fifty years ago.

GLEN:       I think we were just young. I told you he passed.

SANDY:      When?

GLEN:       When I tried coming home the other night. I was trying to get a change of clothes to wear to the visitation.

SANDY:      This is the first I'm hearing about it.

GLEN:       No, it isn't.

SANDY:      You probably told me in a voicemail I didn't listen to. So how was it? The visitation.

GLEN:       Ghost town.

SANDY:      I suppose by a hundred and four, you've outlived everyone.

GLEN:       I met his daughter. She's eighty. I told her how he always reserved this date for us— well, back when we were still renting.

SANDY:      Did you tell her about the to-do lists?

GLEN:       No. That was just part of the deal.

SANDY:      Mmhm.

GLEN:       He barely charged us anything.

SANDY:      And you spent every anniversary fixing something.

GLEN:       Well, paid off in the end.

SANDY:      Yeah, not a bad place to land when you get the boot. So whaddaya say? I take the house, you take the cottage, let's call the lawyer and get this thing over with.

GLEN:       Sandy.

SANDY:      I won't ask for child support. They're forty-five and forty-nine, they can take care of themselves.

GLEN:       Come on—

SANDY:      Everything else, fifty-fifty. Where do I sign?

GLEN:       We can work this out.

SANDY:      Oh! Can we?

GLEN:       Look. I know I have a few things to work on.

SANDY:      A few? That's the understatement of the century.

GLEN:       But it's not just me. Listen, Stacey and I have been talking—

SANDY:      Glen—

GLEN:       And Greg too.

SANDY:      Drop it.

GLEN:       We all agree it would be for the best—

SANDY:      (*Quite hot.*) You keep this up, I will march right out of here as fast as I came.

GLEN:       (*Backs off.*) Okay. …Okay.

> Beat. SANDY *looks towards the Dempsey cottage.*

SANDY:      So. You've seen Patty Dempsey?

GLEN:       A bunch of times.

SANDY:      (*With innuendo.*) Oh?

GLEN:       At yoga.

SANDY:      Patty goes to yoga?

GLEN:       She got a new hip.

SANDY:      What, another one?

GLEN:       After they did the opposite knee, she needed that hip done too.

SANDY:      Doesn't she also have a rod in her arm?

GLEN:    And a plate in her shoulder. Oh, and she got a pacemaker. It's like watching the Tin Man do yoga. She got Stacey's email disinviting her to the party, so I had to tell her what's up. "Never woulda seen it coming," she said. "Glen and Sandy? Not in a million years."

SANDY:    Well, you never know what's really going on with people, do you?

GLEN:    Sure don't.

SANDY:    So, are you two hooking up, or what?

GLEN:    Excuse me?

SANDY:    It's been a few years since Murray died. She should be raring to go by now. *(Getting off the deck and calling over.)* Hey, Patty! You sleeping with my husband?

GLEN:    Sandy.

SANDY:    He's all yours, sweetheart!

GLEN:    Shh!

SANDY:    If you can stand him, you can have him!

GLEN:    Oh my God.

SANDY:    No, you should go for it. Patty always had a thing for you.

GLEN:    I beg your pardon?

SANDY:    Oh, don't pretend you didn't know. Whenever we'd get together with them, she'd be all: "Are you gonna give me a deal on my new car, Glen?" "I baked this pie for you, Glen." "You're such a good golfer, Glen." Or my favourite: *(Holding mime cards.)* "I'll make it hearts—for my partner." And she wasn't playing with Murray.

GLEN:        You jealous?

SANDY:       Jealous? I'm telling you to go for it.

GLEN:        I don't want to date Patty Dempsey.

SANDY:       Why not? She's very attractive—for a bionic
             woman.

GLEN:        I don't want to date anyone.

SANDY:       Well, you could—

GLEN:        No, thank you.

SANDY:       If you want.

GLEN:        I don't.

SANDY:       I'm just saying—

GLEN:        *(A bit too hot.)* Can we please drop it?

SANDY:       Excuse me. I thought we were talking.

GLEN:        *(Quick beat.)* Wait. Are you?

SANDY:       Am I what?

GLEN:        Dating someone.

SANDY:       Wouldn't you like to know?

GLEN:        Is that who you were having dinner with? On
             our anniversary?

SANDY:       *(Laughing.)* Ohhhh, who's jealous now?

GLEN:        It's not funny.

SANDY:       You and I are not together. Who I have dinner
             with is my prerogative.

GLEN:        Oh! So you've got another man then?

SANDY:       I didn't say that.

GLEN:            So you don't?

SANDY:           Didn't say that either.

GLEN:            Sandy!

SANDY:           Would you calm down?

> *GLEN goes into yoga mountain pose again, breathing in and out hard.*

                 What is that?

GLEN:            Yoga.

SANDY:           That doesn't look like yoga.

GLEN:            Well, it is.

SANDY:           I don't think so.

GLEN:            It is yoga. It's breathing. It helps me calm down.

SANDY:           I don't think you're doing it right.

GLEN:            I'm the one taking the class! I would know!

SANDY:           Don't think it's working.

GLEN:            *(He drops the yoga.)* Does our rule apply here?

SANDY:           What rule?

GLEN:            The rule we made. You know, if either of us was ever interested in someone else.

SANDY:           What are you talking about?

GLEN:            If you or me were ever thinking about… extra-marital activities, we agreed to be up front about it.

SANDY:           Was I part of this conversation?

GLEN:       Yes. It was your idea. Right here, if memory serves.

SANDY:      When?

GLEN:       Years ago. And I'm asking if it still applies, under the current circumstances, cuz if it does, you are required to tell me about your boyfriend.

SANDY:      I don't have a boyfriend.

GLEN:       Oh. Well, never mind then.

SANDY:      I have several.

GLEN:       Oh my God!

SANDY:      You are making this rule thing up.

GLEN:       I'm not. It was the year of that heat wave, remember?

SANDY:      It's July. There was a heat wave every year.

GLEN:       You were teaching summer school.

SANDY:      I did that for what, ten years?

GLEN:       I was trying to quit smoking.

SANDY:      You did that for fifteen.

GLEN:       The Nicorette anniversary.

SANDY:      Ohhh, I know what happened that year.

GLEN:       No, before all that. We made an agreement. You were there, I was here. And it was seven hundred degrees…

> *Transition to thirty-seven years ago: SANDY and GLEN's 13th anniversary. It's midday and the sun is blazing. The portable stereo quietly plays music from this year in the 1980s.*
>
> *GLEN sits on the edge of the deck, gets out a pack of Nicorette and takes one. SANDY has popped her head inside the cottage to get a folder of papers and a red pen. She closes the door. They are both extremely hot.*

SANDY: Kill me now!

GLEN: Go back inside.

SANDY: I can't even breathe in there; it's hotter than the devil's nut sack.

GLEN: It's not the heat, you know. It's the humidity.

SANDY: *(Noticing the Nicorette.)* How many of those are you allowed to have?

GLEN: *(Reading the package.)* Nine to twelve.

SANDY: A day? How many are you on?

GLEN: It's fine. As long as I don't murder the anti-smoking people who convinced Stacey I was gonna die if I had one more cigarette.

SANDY: Someday you'll be old and grey and thankful you gave it up.

GLEN: Or old and grey, thinking: "Nope, shoulda kept smoking."

> *GLEN starts bouncing up and down on deck boards to try to find a rotten one. He does this through the scene. SANDY is now marking her papers.*

SANDY: What are you doing?

GLEN:        Looking for that board.

SANDY:       What board?

GLEN:        The one Patrick asked me to replace.

SANDY:       On the to-do list?

GLEN:        He says there's a rotten board out here. He doesn't want someone to fall through. He just didn't say where.

SANDY:       You don't need to do it today.

GLEN:        I said I would. Part of the deal.

SANDY:       *(Fans herself with the papers.)* Uuuuggh!

GLEN:        Go back in the lake.

SANDY:       No, I have to finish this marking. I swear, I am never teaching summer school again.

GLEN:        You didn't have to do it this year.

SANDY:       That's not what you said when we renovated the kitchen. *(Back to her papers.)* These kids, though! Not the sharpest tools in the shed.

GLEN:        Probably why they're in summer school.

SANDY:       If we're not careful, this'll be Greg, you know.

GLEN:        Oh, it will not.

SANDY:       He's behind, Glen. You weren't at the parent-teacher interview.

GLEN:        Cuz I was working?

SANDY:       Do you know how embarrassing it is, as a teacher, to sit there and hear them call your son a "problem child"?

GLEN:        So he's not a fan of the whole school thing—

SANDY:      Not a fan? He killed their classroom hamster.

GLEN:       He was trying to give it fresh air. How was he supposed to know that eagle was close by?

SANDY:      Before September, you have to talk to him. He needs to pull up his socks.

GLEN:       In Grade four?

SANDY:      Yes.

GLEN:       Okay. I'll talk to him.

SANDY:      And Stacey too.

GLEN:       What do you want me to say to her?

SANDY:      Stop being a little bitch.

GLEN:       Hey!

SANDY:      Oh no, she's sweet with you. Daddy's little girl. But with me? Nightmare.

GLEN:       She's twelve years old. Did you get along with your mother at that age?

SANDY:      Yes. I had the decency to wait till I was thirteen to hate her.

                *GLEN stands on one spot and bounces, contemplating whether or not this is the rotten board.*

        That the one?

GLEN:       *(Bounce, bounce, bounce.)* …Nope. *(He looks for another board and feels nauseous.)* Is that lunch sitting right with you?

SANDY:      Yeah, why, are you sick?

GLEN:       Just hot. *(He pops another piece of Nicorette.)*

| | |
|---|---|
| SANDY: | (*Referring to a paper.*) Grade eleven and they don't know parts of speech. I say: "Underline the verb in the following sentence: Juliet falls in love with Romeo at a masked ball." And this boy underlines, "Juliet love Romeo ball." |
| | *GLEN laughs.* |
| | No verbs. |
| GLEN: | Love? |
| SANDY: | No, "falls" is the verbs. She *falls* in love. |
| GLEN: | No one's ever asked me what a verb is when they're buying a car, you know. |
| SANDY: | No, they probably ask Bill. |
| GLEN: | God, I hope not. I wouldn't wanna know what verbs he'd come up with. |
| | *GLEN's mood shifts. A big exhale or sigh.* |
| SANDY: | What's wrong? |
| GLEN: | Nothing. |
| SANDY: | Your stomach? |
| GLEN: | No, it's just… Never mind. |
| SANDY: | …No, what? |
| | *He turns off the radio and joins her at the table.* |
| GLEN: | You know the other night when I went back to work after supper? |
| SANDY: | Yeah…? |
| GLEN: | And when I came home, I was acting kinda weird? |

SANDY:        You're always acting weird. What happened?

GLEN.         I was in the office doing paperwork, and I heard something out in the showroom, so I went to check. And it was Bill…with a woman. Not Sharon.

SANDY:        What were they doing? *(A look from GLEN.)* In the dealership!?

GLEN:         On the hood of a brand-new '88 Buick Century.

SANDY:        I hope she bought it.

GLEN:         I talked to him about it the next morning. He said it was a momentary lapse in judgment.

SANDY:        Last time he had a momentary lapse in judgment, he was married to Diane.

GLEN:         Not the last time.

SANDY:        Ohhh! *(What a mess.)* Does Sharon know he's running around on her?

GLEN:         No. *(Getting up.)* And she doesn't need to. He told me he'd stop.

SANDY:        And you believe him? We have to tell her.

GLEN:         No, see, this is why I didn't say anything.

SANDY:        What if he gets something and gives it to her?

GLEN:         He says he's careful. Forget I said anything.

SANDY:        Glen.

GLEN:         We saw how ugly things got with Debra and Richard.

SANDY:        That was different.

GLEN:    Those poor kids caught in the middle; we don't need that again. I got it off my chest. So, there. We'll leave it at that.

SANDY:    If you were cheating on me, I would want to know.

GLEN:    Well, good thing I'm not.

SANDY:    I'm saying *if*.

GLEN:    Honey, I would never do that.

SANDY:    (*Getting up to join him.*) But it happens— clearly. So let's agree, okay? If you're thinking about it, do me a favour and tell me first.

GLEN:    What?

SANDY:    Give me a heads up. Before you're banging some strange woman on the hood of a car. And I'll do the same for you.

GLEN:    Okie-doke.

> **A quick transition back to the present: evening light.** *They are standing around where they were when GLEN introduced "the rule."*

GLEN:    See? That's the rule.

SANDY:    Wait. That's it?

GLEN:    Yes. We agreed on it.

SANDY:    No, you said, "Okie-doke." I don't think that holds up in court.

GLEN:    I'm saying we were on the same page about this.

SANDY:    But that wasn't the end of the conversation.

GLEN:        Oh! So you remember this now?

SANDY:       As a matter of fact, I do. I said, "Let's tell each other before we cheat," you said, "Okie-doke," and I said something like…

> ***Another quick transition back to the past.*** *The blazing sun of their 13th anniversary; we pick up the scene around where we left off. GLEN bounces on the boards. SANDY gets back to her marking.*

It's the lying that hurts people. If you're honest, you can nip it in the bud before you do anything stupid. Or if you simply must act on it, at least get my approval first.

GLEN:        Your approval?

SANDY:       Yes.

GLEN:        What, should I bring the woman's photo? Her credit score? What will you need?

SANDY:       Honesty.

GLEN:        So as long as we ask permission, it's okay?

SANDY:       No! I don't know. But I'd rather we get our jollies with other people and stay married than sneak around behind each other's backs.

GLEN:        Are you a swinger?

SANDY:       What?

GLEN:        Is that what you're trying to tell me?

SANDY:       No, I am not a swinger.

GLEN:        *(Sitting.)* Cuz you know who is? The people on the corner.

SANDY:       Who?

GLEN:    At home, the new neighbours. The Blacks.

SANDY:    Robert and Susan?

GLEN:    Roger and Suzanne.

SANDY:    Roger. (*Her Suzanne impression we heard earlier.*) And Suzanne!

GLEN:    Ha!

SANDY:    They're swingers?

GLEN:    According to Rog. He said they belong to a group. I think he was scoping us out.

SANDY:    Oh my God.

GLEN:    He gave me a pamphlet and everything—

SANDY:    They have pamphlets?

GLEN:    He said we should come see for ourselves.

SANDY:    If I'm gonna knock boots with another man, I'll find someone sexier than Roger Black.

GLEN:    Ooof. (*His stomach again. He stands.*)

SANDY:    Go have some water.

GLEN:    I'm fine. (*He pops another Nicorette.*)

SANDY:    (*Joining him standing.*) Do you want to go?

GLEN:    Where?

SANDY:    To the swingers' club?

GLEN:    (*Thinks about it.*) Uhhh…

SANDY:    Oh my God, do you want to sleep with Suzanne Black?

GLEN:    Not Suzanne.

SANDY:        No, she'd talk your ear off.

                   *GLEN laughs. In this, a quick transition back to the present—50th Anniversary.*

GLEN:         Ha! Roger and Suzanne were swingers. I'd forgotten all about that. Do you think they still are?

SANDY:        At this age? Perish the thought.

GLEN:         So! Based on all that: if you're seeing someone, you have to tell me about him.

SANDY:        What?

GLEN:         That's what you proposed. And I'm allowed to give him the thumbs up or down.

SANDY:        Any "rules" you think we had are now moot.

GLEN:         We are still married, dear.

SANDY:        You're interrupting again.

GLEN:         That was the whole conversation.

SANDY:        Oh, it was not.

GLEN:         Well, you get the gist.

SANDY:        No, don't you recall what happened next?

GLEN:         Never mind that.

SANDY:        Come on, since we're reminiscing—

GLEN:         We don't need to go over all that.

SANDY:        Why not?

GLEN:         It's irrelevant.

SANDY:        It's very relevant.

GLEN:        How so?

SANDY:       Proves you were nuts even back then. So! You kept popping Nicorette and I said:

> *Quick transition back to their 13th Anniversary, again picking up the scene approximately where they stopped.* GLEN *is popping a Nicorette. He's increasingly frustrated by the boards, bouncing harder on them to find the rotten one.*

SANDY:       That's what's wrong with your stomach.

GLEN:        It's just the heat.

SANDY:       *(Mocking him from earlier. Back to her marking.)* It's not the heat. It's the humidity!

GLEN:        Where the hell is this thing? *(The board.)*

SANDY:       You know, I hope Sharon's doing the same thing to Bill.

GLEN:        What, two-timing him?

SANDY:       Why not? She's got that gorgeous body, even after three kids. Sure, she still dresses like a hooker, but she's family and we love her and I hope she's got some hunk on the side.

GLEN:        Oh, so it's okay to cheat if you're being cheated on?

SANDY:       That's not what I'm saying.

GLEN:        What's good for the goose?

SANDY:       No.

GLEN:        So what are you saying?

SANDY:        I don't know. I'm sick of all these wonderful
              women we know getting their hearts broken
              by their loser husbands.

GLEN:         Bill is not a loser.

SANDY:        He's sure as hell acting like one.

GLEN:         Your sister and Richard, that was a two-way
              street.

SANDY:        Richard is a monster.

GLEN:         Well, Debra's no peach.

SANDY:        Excuse me?

GLEN:         She did very well for herself in the divorce.

SANDY:        After what he put her through, she earned
              every red cent.

GLEN:         *(To the boards.)* Oh, come on!

SANDY:        Tell Pat you can't do it.

GLEN:         No.

SANDY:        You're not feeling well.

GLEN:         I'm gonna get it.

SANDY:        You'll overheat.

GLEN:         I said I'd find it. Unlike all the loser husbands
              we know, when I make a promise, I stick to it.

              *Crack! A board gives way and GLEN's leg
              falls through the deck.*

SANDY:        I think that's the one.

GLEN:         Ow.

SANDY:        *(Coming over.)* You okay?

GLEN:        No. Ah. Ow!

SANDY:       *(Helping him out of the hole.)* Here.

GLEN:        Do you think it's bleeding?

SANDY:       No.

GLEN:        I can't look.

SANDY:       You're fine.

GLEN:        I'm not fine. It hurts. *(He's out of the hole and supporting his weight on the table.)*

SANDY:       Where?

GLEN:        My foot! *(She starts to roll up his pant leg, but he looks away.)* Is there blood?

SANDY:       Do you really want to know?

GLEN:        Oh God, I'm gonna be sick.

SANDY:       Not on these! *(She quickly moves her papers out of the way.)* What do you need?

GLEN:        A smoke!

SANDY:       For your foot?

GLEN:        I don't know. *(He tries putting weight on it, but it buckles.)* Ahhhhh.

SANDY:       Okay, we're going to emerg.

*She helps him hobble to the side.*

GLEN:        I will never cheat on you.

SANDY:       All right.

GLEN:        Please don't cheat on me.

SANDY:       Yep, here we go.

GLEN:       I am not a loser.

SANDY:      Good stuff.

GLEN:       (*He stops.*) Oh, God.

SANDY:      What?

*He leans over the rail to barf.*

***A slightly longer transition back to the present: evening light on their 50th anniversary.*** *The broken board restores. GLEN and SANDY can be in different places on the stage from where this memory began.*

SANDY:      You see? Nuts.

GLEN:       I had heatstroke, a broken foot, and was overdosing on nicotine.

SANDY:      I rest my case.

GLEN:       So. Are you going to tell me who you were having dinner with or not?

SANDY:      ...Not.

GLEN:       What ever happened to honesty? Communication? All the stuff we used to work on?

SANDY:      I don't know. You tell me.

GLEN:       Look, I am trying here. But we can't sort things out between us if we're keeping secrets.

SANDY:      It wasn't a date. My dinner.

GLEN:       No?

SANDY:      No. It was a...a meeting.

GLEN:        With who?

SANDY:       My old publisher.

GLEN:        What, did he just happen to be in town, or—?

SANDY:       No, they want me to come out of retirement;
             write a new book.

GLEN:        …Oh.

SANDY:       He thinks it would sell. You know, if I follow
             the formula. "The demand is there!"

GLEN:        …I see.

SANDY:       So…did you stick to it?

GLEN:        To what?

SANDY:       To what you said. You were barfing your guts
             out swearing you'd never cheat.

GLEN:        Of course. God, Sandy, I know I haven't been
             the perfect husband, but I never did that.

SANDY:       All right.

GLEN:        It never even crossed my mind.

SANDY:       (That's a bit overkill.) Okay.

GLEN:        It's true!

SANDY:       Are you trying to tell me you never so much
             as thought about it?

GLEN:        Never.

SANDY:       In fifty years?

GLEN:        No.

SANDY:       Never looked at another woman.

GLEN:         Not like that.

SANDY:        Oh, get real.

GLEN:         What, so you did? Think about it? Other men?

SANDY:        I'm human.

GLEN:         Oh! And is that all it was, thinking? Or is there anything else I should know?

SANDY:        Why are we even talking about this?

GLEN:         You brought it up.

SANDY:        You did.

GLEN:         Just answer the question then. Did you… stray? …Oh my God, you did.

SANDY:        I never said—

GLEN:         With who? Do I know him? I don't wanna know. Yes, I do. No, I don't. God, I don't know!

SANDY:        Would you chill out?

GLEN:         I'm chill. I've walked sixty thousand steps in the past six days. I am chill.

SANDY:        Okay, I'm going to the washroom. (*She heads toward the door.*)

GLEN:         What?

SANDY:        Before I hit the road.

GLEN:         Hit the road? We haven't had our conversation yet.

SANDY:        What have we been doing since I got here?

GLEN:          Chatting, but not about what we need to discuss.

SANDY:         *(Firmly.)* No, thank you.

GLEN:          Was it someone you taught with? Mr. Peterson? Mr. Lee? Monsieur LaRue?

SANDY:         Monsieur LaRue?!

GLEN:          When was it? This affair.

SANDY:         It wasn't an affair.

GLEN:          Or whatever it was.

SANDY:         It was nothing. You and I, we weren't in a good place and I— Oh, who cares?

GLEN:          I care.

SANDY:         It is ancient history, Glen.

GLEN:          When?

SANDY:         Twenty-five years ago!

GLEN:          *(Beat.)* Oh.

SANDY:         Excuse me.

        *SANDY goes inside. GLEN is left alone.*

GLEN:          I shoulda known…

        ***Transition to twenty-five years ago: the Goldens' 25th anniversary.*** *It's a bit earlier in the day—around 5:30 pm—and a different quality of light from the present. A cell phone rings. GLEN takes a flip-phone from the late 1990s out of his pocket and answers.*

GLEN:  Glen Golden. (*But it's still ringing. He pushes a button.*) Hello? (*Still ringing. He tries another button.*) Hello? (*Another ring. Another button.*) Ah. Bill? …Hey, yeah, I'm still getting used to this thing. So what'd they say? …Uh huh. …Uh huh. …Uh huh! So should we counteroffer? …No, God, not that high! …Yeah, yeah, spend money to make money. …Okay, go back to them with that and—

> *SANDY enters from the cottage, trying to clasp a silver necklace around her neck.*

Bill? Did I lose you? Bill?

SANDY:  I am going to throw that thing in the lake.

GLEN:  We're negotiating this new piece of land.

SANDY:  It can't wait till you're back?

GLEN:  Someone else is interested, we gotta move.

SANDY:  Let Bill deal with it.

GLEN:  He is.

SANDY:  The only reason you keep buying land and opening new dealerships is so Bill can pay his ever-expanding alimony.

GLEN:  Not the only reason.

SANDY:  No?

GLEN:  We sure as hell need the income.

SANDY:  It is just for a year. We'll be fine.

GLEN:  (*Unconvinced.*) Sure.

SANDY:  If I don't do this now, when? I always said I would write a book, but then a baby comes along and another and poof! Twenty-five years go by and I haven't put pen to paper.

GLEN:      Did you need to quit teaching, though?

SANDY:     I didn't quit.

GLEN:      Unpaid leave, same difference.

SANDY:     I need time to focus on my book. Everyone in my writing group says it's an amazing idea. The one guy, Daniel, he's an incredible writer; he said if it's as good as it sounds, I'll make it onto Oprah's book club. And then you can build all the car dealerships your little heart desires.

GLEN:      *(Noticing her struggle with the necklace.)* Need a hand?

SANDY:     Yes.

           *He helps her.*

           Our reservation's at six, you know?

GLEN:      Where are we going?

SANDY:     *(Reminding him, yet again.)* The new restaurant. At the Inn?

GLEN:      Right. *(The necklace is on now.)* Lemme see?

           *She does.*

           Nice. Pure silver.

SANDY:     Uh huh.

GLEN:      Silver Anniversary…?

SANDY:     Got it.

GLEN:      Do you like it?

SANDY:     Yeah. I wouldn't have picked it for myself, but… Go change.

GLEN:       For what?

SANDY:      Dinner.

GLEN:       I can't wear this?

SANDY:      It's a nice place.

GLEN:       How nice?

SANDY:      Nice. I told you!

GLEN:       Okay! Jeez. I've got other stuff going on.

SANDY:      Don't I know it. You know, I don't understand why you're buying more property for the business when we agreed we were saving up to buy this place.

GLEN:       The cottage isn't time-sensitive, this is. Pat Hargrave said we can figure out a deal here whenever. Plus, it's kinda hard to save for a cottage when you just gave up your income.

*The cell phone rings again.*

SANDY:      Leave it.

GLEN:       It'll be Bill. *(He answers.)* Hey, sorry, the reception out here— What? Oh. *(To SANDY.)* It's Greg. *(Phone.)* I don't know… I don't know. *(To SANDY.)* He wants to know what temperature to cook the lasagna at.

SANDY:      What lasagna?

GLEN:       It was in the freezer.

SANDY:      No, that's not for him. There's food in the fridge.

GLEN:       *(Phone.)* Your mother says eat something in the fridge. *(To SANDY.)* He ate it all.

SANDY:      What?

GLEN:       *(Phone.)* Talk to her.

SANDY:      *(She takes the phone.)* You ate everything? *(To GLEN.)* Go change your clothes. *(Phone.)* No, that lasagna's for Grandma. …Grandma Golden! Everything in the freezer's for her, so don't touch it.

GLEN:       Bill might be calling back.

SANDY:      Oh my God. *(Phone.)* Go to the store, Gregory. …Well, get your sister to drive you. …Then walk!

> She hangs up and puts the phone on the table.

Where did we go wrong?

GLEN:       Maybe if you didn't keep the fridge stocked with their favourite foods, they'd move out.

SANDY:      Oh, this is not my fault.

GLEN:       It's mine?

SANDY:      I told you to give him a job.

GLEN:       He refuses to work for me. And Stacey, she's still living home because of you.

SANDY:      What?

GLEN:       She had one foot out the door, and you told her to go back to university. For the third time.

SANDY:      At least she's doing something.

GLEN:       Why can't she drive him to the store?

SANDY:      She's at that Tom guy's place.

GLEN:        Tim.

SANDY:       Tim.

GLEN:        Again?

SANDY:       If we're lucky, she'll move in with him. *(To God.)* Please!

GLEN:        That's what Greg needs, you know: a girlfriend.

SANDY:       Oh, so he can become her problem?

GLEN:        No, it might motivate him to get his act together. When I was his age, we were married.

SANDY:       And you're planning on getting your act together, when?

GLEN:        Would you stop?

SANDY:       What?

GLEN:        Your little jabs.

SANDY:       We're leaving in five minutes.

GLEN:        What about one of the young ladies in your writers' group?

SANDY:       What?

GLEN:        For Greg. You said it's you and this Daniel guy and a bunch of young women. Introduce him to one of them.

SANDY:       I'm not so sure they're what Greg's looking for.

GLEN:        Why not?

SANDY:       I don't know if it's a *girlfriend* he wants.

GLEN:        What?

SANDY:       Could be why he's so depressed.

GLEN:        He's not depressed. He smokes too much weed.

SANDY:       Glen, he takes after your mother. And you.

GLEN:        I'm not depressed. I'm surrounded by assholes.

SANDY:       Oh!

GLEN:        And Greg's not gay. He took wood shop.

SANDY:       Well then, never mind. Would you please go change your clothes? *(She opens the door for him.)*

GLEN:        This is all I brought.

SANDY:       Oh my God.

GLEN:        It's fine; you want me to tuck this in?

SANDY:       Oh my God.

GLEN:        What, are they not gonna let me in the restaurant?

SANDY:       Oh my God!

> *A quick transition, back to the present. 50th anniversary. SANDY closes the door, coming out of the washroom.*

SANDY:       There's no hand soap by the sink.

GLEN:        What?

SANDY:       In the bathroom. What are you using to wash your hands?

GLEN:        Was it Daniel? From your writers' group?

SANDY:        You are not still thinking about that, are you?

GLEN:         "An incredible writer." That's not all he was.

SANDY:        I go inside for two minutes and you're out here strolling down memory lane again?

GLEN:         This changes things—about that night. Here, I always thought the problem was me. Working too much, not communicating, in a rut.

SANDY:        You were.

GLEN:         But now I learn you had a little something on the side?

SANDY:        It was a dumb crush; we hung out, but nothing ever happened. He made me feel smart, he made me feel special.

GLEN:         And I didn't?

SANDY:        Not then, no.

GLEN:         I gave you a silver necklace and you didn't even care.

SANDY:        I didn't want a necklace, Glen.

GLEN:         What did you want?

SANDY:        I wanted…change!

              *Instant transition. Back to their 25th anniversary.*

GLEN:         I can't change! This is the shirt I've got!

SANDY:        I'm not talking about your shirt! I'm talking about my life. Is this all it is? Kids who won't leave home, and a mother-in-law who needs lasagna, and a workaholic husband who can't remember I don't like silver?

GLEN:        What?

SANDY:       I am trying to shake things up. I thought this weekend might help, but nope, here we are—again.

GLEN:        We always come here.

SANDY:       I don't mean here, Glen. I mean *here*: at each other's throats.

GLEN:        You're the one barking at me.

SANDY:       Yeah, and I don't want to do it anymore! I just read a whole chapter today in one of those books about marriage I got: "How to Break Unhealthy Patterns." I told myself this anniversary was a chance for us to reset: a dip in the lake, a nice dinner, maybe even a roll in the hay—

GLEN:        You want to have sex?

SANDY:       Would you listen?

GLEN:        No, forget dinner.

SANDY:       Glen.

GLEN:        It's been a while, but let's go!

SANDY:       Glen.

GLEN:        I am up for it, darlin'—any time.

SANDY:       To be up for it, you'd have to get it up for it, and that's the problem. *(Quick beat.)* Shit.

GLEN:        You might want to read that chapter again.

             *His phone rings. It's on the table. A stare down. After a couple rings, he answers.*

             Bill? Hey listen, it's our anniversary, we're on our way to dinner—

SANDY:        I'm gonna go.

GLEN:         *(To SANDY.)* I'm coming. I'll wear the shirt I
              wore yesterday.

SANDY:        Not to the restaurant.

GLEN:         *(Phone.)* Hang on.

SANDY:        I'm going somewhere else.

GLEN:         *(Phone.)* Bill, I'll call you back. *(Hangs up.)*

SANDY:        Somewhere without you.

              **Transition back to the present: their
              50th anniversary.**

GLEN:         Did you go see him that night? Daniel?

SANDY:        You know I didn't.

GLEN:         Where did you go?

SANDY:        My sister's.

GLEN:         Oh, right. I can only imagine what she had to
              say.

SANDY:        She said we could work it out. "Just a rough
              patch. Talk in the morning. You're not done
              yet."

GLEN:         Yeah? And she was right.

SANDY:        *(As if.)* Yeah!

GLEN:         No, we talked—and we kept talking. I read
              all those books on marriage too. We figured
              things out. We were good after that.

SANDY:        For a time.

GLEN:         For a long time. And we got that other book.
              Remember that one?

SANDY:      What?

GLEN:       The Sex Book.

SANDY:      Oh, Glen—

GLEN:       We brought it here that time?

SANDY:      Is this why you wanted me to come?

GLEN:       What?

SANDY:      Try and convince me we had fifty years of marital bliss?

GLEN:       That's not what I'm doing.

SANDY:      (*Sarcastic.*) Right.

GLEN:       It wasn't all misery, either. We had some tough times, but we always made it through.

SANDY:      And you think that's going to happen again, don't you?

GLEN:       Honey, I need to come home. The kids and I, we're worried about you.

SANDY:      I am fine.

GLEN:       You're not fine. You couldn't remember Suzanne's name.

SANDY:      I could never remember anyone's name.

GLEN:       The other night, I told you Pat Hargrave died.

SANDY:      You didn't.

GLEN:       You forgot all about going to dinner with your publisher.

SANDY:      Because I thought you were dying. You're the one who can't remember anything.

GLEN:          (*Pulling out a chair.*) Let's just have a seat and talk it through.

SANDY:          I don't have to put up with this shit. (*Starts to get her purse.*)

GLEN:          Sandy, come on.

SANDY:          Trick me into coming and then you start up with this again.

GLEN:          Honey—

SANDY:          Don't honey me.

*She starts to go, SL—opposite from where she came in.*

GLEN:          You can't go that way.

SANDY:          I'll go whichever way I please.

GLEN:          No, the mud.

SANDY:          What mud?

GLEN:          (*Goes to grab her.*) Come here.

SANDY:          Get your hands off me! We are done, do you hear me? Done. (*Starts to go.*)

GLEN:          Wait, wait, wait—

SANDY:          (*Turning back.*) Happy Fucking Anniversary.

*She exits. Music kicks in.*

GLEN:          Sandy!

*He starts to follow her off.*

*Blackout.*

*End of Act One.*

## Act Two

*The present, about twenty minutes after the end of Act One. The sun is starting to set now. Sound of the lake and birds. SANDY enters from inside wearing different clothes; something more casual, which she found at the cottage. She's carrying a small glass of water. She looks out at the lake, then rediscovers the bottle of wine, off to the side where GLEN put it down earlier. She looks at the label, as though seeing it's her favourite for the first time.*

SANDY:          Huh.

*She tosses the rest of her water over the side of the deck and pours herself some wine. GLEN enters from inside. He's also changed his clothes. He moves very gingerly; his back is seized up.*

SANDY:          What's the matter with you?

GLEN:          I wiped out. In the mud? Chasing after you?

SANDY:          I know that, Glen. I was there. I'm asking if you threw your back out.

GLEN:          I did something. (*He sits, slowly. It hurts.*) You found clean clothes?

SANDY:          In the dresser. I didn't exactly have mud wrestling on tonight's bingo card, and yet…

GLEN:            Thank you for helping me up. *(Beat.)* So. Have you cooled down?

SANDY:           Have you?

GLEN:            Are we ready to talk? Like reasonable people?

> *SANDY stares out at the lake, giving him the silent treatment. She sips her wine.*

How's the wine?

SANDY:           Fine.

GLEN:            Do you want some food?

SANDY:           Not hungry.

GLEN:            Oh. Well, I could eat.

SANDY:           Go ahead.

> *He stands, with difficulty, and starts to go in.*

GLEN:            Are you sure you don't want anything?

SANDY:           What are the options?

GLEN:            Wieners, beans, or the chef's specialty.

SANDY:           I'll take the special. *(Before he's through the door.)* Did they have this in town? *(The wine.)*

GLEN:            No. I had to go to the big liquor store.

SANDY:           Oh. It's good.

GLEN:            Yeah.

SANDY:           This one's my favourite.

GLEN:            I know.

*GLEN goes inside. SANDY goes to pour a bit more, but notices something under the bottle. She puts her glass down, and picks up a wood burnt sign that says, "THE GOLDEN'S." She holds it up towards the door…*

***Transition to late at night, it's dark out on the deck, but there are lights on inside the cottage. The candle in the lantern is glowing, and possibly the outdoor lights. It's twenty years ago: SANDY and GLEN's 30th anniversary.***

GLEN:    *(Off.)* Ready or not, here I come!

*SANDY puts the sign down. She looks for a place to hide. Through the windows, we can see GLEN moving around, looking for her.*

Hellooo?

*SANDY hides behind the barbecue. GLEN comes through the door. He's carrying a book clearly titled, "MARRIED SEX." He looks for her around one side of the cottage, then the other.*

Come out, come out, wherever you are… You wascally wabbit. Ha!

*He finds her behind the barbecue.*

SANDY:    Ahhhh!

GLEN:    You want to have sex behind the barbecue?

SANDY:    *(Coming out from there.)* No!

GLEN:    But it says: *(Referencing the book.)* "Play hide and seek with your partner to find a fun new place where you've never made love."

SANDY:        Out here.

GLEN:         On the deck? What if someone sees us?

SANDY:        Like who?

GLEN:         The Dempseys. They have a clear sightline.

SANDY:        I bet Patty would like that.

GLEN:         Or a boat could go by?

SANDY:        It's dark, Glen. Come on! Thirty anniversaries coming here and it's the first one when we own the joint. *(Referring to the book.)* It says to be adventurous.

GLEN:         Does it say to get a tetanus shot?

SANDY:        *(Playfully—in an accent.)* Oh, please, my big, strong, handsome man! Make love to me by the light of the moon!

GLEN:         How many of those brownies did you have?

SANDY:        One. It's not even hitting me yet.

GLEN:         *(Yeah, right.)* Okay!

SANDY:        It's not. Greg said it takes forty-five minutes to kick in. Are you sure you don't want one? Might help you relax…

GLEN:         I am relaxed.

SANDY:        Ha.

GLEN:         It's this father-of-the-bride speech. I've got nothing.

SANDY:        You have a few days to figure it out.

GLEN:         But I have no clue what to say.

SANDY:      "Congratulations"? "I can't believe my little girl's all grown up"? "Tim, welcome to the family"? Make some joke about how his dumb boss at Golden Motors doesn't pay him enough, so you had to foot the bill for the wedding.

GLEN:       Oh, that's good.

SANDY:      Say you're happy to finally have a son who golfs.

GLEN:       See? You're the writer. You should do it.

SANDY:      Nope. I've been told my job is to wear beige and shut up.

GLEN:       Stacey doesn't want her successful author mother to speak?

SANDY:      Apparently not. It's not as if her fancy PhD friends would be impressed with my literary credentials.

GLEN:       You don't know that.

SANDY:      They don't read the kind of books I write.

GLEN:       They might. Oh! Did I tell you this? There was a young woman waiting for her new car the other day and she was reading one of yours.

SANDY:      Which one?

GLEN:       Uh, there's a lady on the cover. And a guy with no shirt on, like: (*His Fabio impression.*)

SANDY:      That's all of them. Remember when I thought I was going to be the next Margaret Atwood? Look at me now.

GLEN:       A success. We bought the cottage! Would you rather go back to teaching?

SANDY:      No!

GLEN:       The woman with your book, I told her: "You know who wrote that? My wife," and she couldn't believe it. "Alexandra Doré is your wife? I freakin' love her!"

SANDY:      Well…she has excellent taste.

GLEN:       Yeah. So you should do the speech.

SANDY:      Stacey wants her dad to do it. I'm going to get drunk before the reception. Or maybe I'll pop one of Greg's brownies.

GLEN:       Don't you dare.

SANDY:      I'm supporting our son's business. He finally found something he's good at.

GLEN:       Dealing drugs.

SANDY:      Baking.

GLEN:       With weed.

SANDY:      It's medicinal.

GLEN:       You got a prescription?

SANDY:      With my sciatica? I could probably get one.

GLEN:       Huh.

SANDY:      It'll be legal soon enough.

GLEN:       I wouldn't put my money on it.

SANDY:      He's happy, Glen. You know what he told me? He feels like he's never measured up to Stacey. She went to university, she's got the big career, she's getting married—

GLEN:       And he's a bipolar bisexual drug dealer.

SANDY:      But he's *our* bipolar bisexual drug dealer.

GLEN:       There's one in every family. Was it good?

SANDY:      The brownie? Delicious. They're on the table…

GLEN:       I don't think I should mix marijuana with my pill.

SANDY:      When did you take it?

GLEN:       Half an hour ago.

SANDY:      Anything yet?

GLEN:       I'll let you know.

SANDY:      You only took one, right?

GLEN:       Yes.

SANDY:      Thank God. We don't need a repeat of your birthday. I was afraid that thing would never go down.

GLEN:       Didn't hear you complaining. *(Looking at the book again.)* What if we did this one instead?

SANDY:      *(She looks.)* What? No! I'm not getting tied up.

GLEN:       *(Pointing to the diagram.)* No, that would be me. And that's you.

SANDY:      *(Sarcastic.)* I'm afraid I forgot my dominatrix outfit at home.

GLEN:       There's gotta be a rope around here somewhere.

SANDY:      Is that what you're into? Getting tied up?

GLEN:       No. But it's no crazier than doing it out in the open for the whole world to see.

SANDY:        Yes, it is. And it's my turn to pick the page!

GLEN:         Can I at least get us a blanket?

SANDY:        This is supposed to be spontaneous. Pretend you're Bill.

GLEN:         I beg your pardon?

SANDY:        No. I just mean he's probably done it outside. On every car lot you own.

GLEN:         Probably. But I think those days are behind him.

SANDY:        Oh, Rochelle keeps him on a tight leash?

GLEN:         Raquel.

SANDY:        Raquel. There's been so many, am I honestly expected to remember her name?

GLEN:         Yes. I think she's a keeper.

SANDY:        Oh! Fourth time's a charm?

GLEN:         Hope so. Bill and I didn't have the greatest role models. For him, the whole marriage thing took a bit of practice.

SANDY:        …You should say that.

GLEN:         What?

SANDY:        In your speech.

GLEN:         "Stacey, Tim: three more times and you'll figure this out."

SANDY:        No, tell them they have to practise. Communication…compromise? All the stuff from the books. And it's better to start learning that stuff now.

GLEN:         I guess.

SANDY:          Tell them…marriage is hard.

GLEN:           Lovely.

SANDY:          Or it takes work. Don't get me wrong: it's worth it. But it ain't easy. Spending the rest of your life with one person? With Tim?

GLEN:           I like Tim.

SANDY:          I love Tim. And he loves Stacey, bless his heart. But I mean, when you stop and think about it, it is wild—hitching yourself to one person, out of all the souls in the entire universe?

GLEN:           Not that wild.

SANDY:          It is! But we all do it—or most people do. Some manage to avoid it; Greg, so far. Some do it multiple times—Bill. Or some are like Debra: she gave it a shot, and it wasn't for her.

GLEN:           You want me to go around the room like that in my speech?

SANDY:          No! I'm just saying the concept is weird.

GLEN:           Marriage?

SANDY:          Yes, or, coupledom or whatever. Like: I am me, right?

GLEN:           Uh huh…

SANDY:          And you are you.

GLEN:           Yep.

SANDY:          But we are also…us. *(She picks up the sign.)* The Goldens. *(Looks at it.)* Wait. The apostrophe's in the wrong spot.

GLEN:           What?

SANDY:    The apostrophe should be after the S. Plural possessive. The Goldens'. *(She does demo with a little click noise to make the apostrophe.)*

GLEN:    Oh.

SANDY:    We can't hang this by the road.

GLEN:    It was a gift.

SANDY:    But what if my copy editor comes to visit?

GLEN:    Pat Hargrave made it for us—with his own two hands.

SANDY:    We'll put it up on the door then.

GLEN:    Deal.

SANDY:    *(Looks at the sign.)* What does this even mean?

GLEN:    It's our cottage?

SANDY:    No, like, "The Goldens." Who is that? You know? Who is "us"?

GLEN:    I think your brownie kicked in.

SANDY:    No. *(Realizes she's high.)* Yeah… Come here, you.

      *He approaches her, with a big grin.*

      What are you smiling at?

GLEN:    It worked. *(His pill.)*

SANDY:    Oh, hello! Do you wanna go inside?

GLEN:    No…your turn to pick the page. Compromise, right?

SANDY:    In that case: get a blanket.

*He hurries inside, taking the book with him. She shouts to him.*

And a pillow for my back! No rope!

*She laughs and looks at the sign.*

**Transition back to the present—GLEN and SANDY's 50th.** *It's now golden hour on the deck.*

*GLEN enters with supper: two bowls of wieners and beans. He is still stiff. SANDY is holding the sign.*

GLEN:        What's so funny?

SANDY:        Nothing. Did you take this down?

GLEN:        Oh, uh… You never really liked it.

SANDY:        I liked it fine.

GLEN:        I just…had a moment.

SANDY:        Pat Hargrave made this for us.

GLEN:        Pat made that?

SANDY:        Yes. With his own two hands.

GLEN:        Oh.

SANDY:        See? I'm an elephant. (*GLEN doesn't get it.*) I don't forget.

GLEN:        Right. Well. Dinner is served.

SANDY:        (*Unimpressed.*) Uh huh… Wine?

GLEN:        What the hell.

*SANDY sees he needs a glass and goes inside. Meanwhile, GLEN, still moving stiffly, goes to the side to light the candle with a BBQ lighter he's brought out. He picks up a small potted plant and brings it back to the table. SANDY re-enters with a glass. GLEN places the plant on the table.*

SANDY:    Oh, much better.

*She pours him wine. They sit down to dinner. Pause.*

GLEN:    So.

SANDY:    So. Are *you* allowed to see the girls?

GLEN:    What?

SANDY:    Stacey refuses to let me see them. I invited them over this week—fun day with Grandma, "let's do our nails," but your daughter wouldn't let them come.

GLEN:    *My* daughter?

SANDY:    She's punishing me because I called off the stupid anniversary party.

GLEN:    I don't think that's it.

SANDY:    Well, have you seen them?

GLEN:    They were here on the weekend. Everyone came up?

SANDY:    ...Right.

GLEN:    Madison drove.

SANDY:    The whole way?

GLEN:    As soon as they got out of the car, Stacey needed a drink. She hasn't told them what's going on, just that...Grandpa's at the cottage. But they're not little girls anymore. And they're not dumb.

SANDY:      They are not.

GLEN:       Chloe sidled up to me and said: "I know what's going on."

SANDY:      Oh?

GLEN:       She goes, "I hope you and Grandma work it out, but you know…marriage!"

SANDY:      Huh.

GLEN:       She swore she'll never get hitched.

SANDY:      That's my girl.

GLEN:       You know all your books end with a wedding, right?

SANDY:      Not all of them.

GLEN:       And then Maddy, she gave me a big hug and asked if I missed you.

SANDY:      Miss me? I'm not dead. What kind of beans are these?

GLEN:       What?

SANDY:      These beans.

GLEN:       I don't know, they're from the can.

SANDY:      You got the No Name beans, didn't you?

GLEN:       I don't know—

SANDY:      You did. Oh, Glen. You can afford the brand-name beans.

GLEN:       All right.

SANDY:      They're not as good.

GLEN:       Okay.

SANDY:          This is pitiful.

GLEN:           You got me! I'm living off No Name beans. I'm wasting away over here. I don't have hand soap. I had to ask a greeter at Walmart where to find the underwear. Our granddaughter asked if I miss you and I start blubbering like a baby. I'm a disaster. Can I please come home now?

SANDY:          Is that what it'll take? For me to see them?

GLEN:           Stacey's…being cautious.

SANDY:          Oh, please.

GLEN:           That time the girls were over and you left the stove on?

SANDY:          Shit happens.

GLEN:           You took them to a movie and drove forty minutes in the wrong direction.

SANDY:          That was Google Map's fault.

GLEN:           She'd feel more comfortable letting them come over if you went and did the tests.

SANDY:          If anyone needs their brain checked, it's her.

GLEN:           Dear—

SANDY:          And you.

GLEN:           We all want you to see the doctor.

SANDY:          Oh, I'm aware. You're all in cahoots. Did the three of you conspire to make that appointment behind my back?

GLEN:           No, that was just me.

SANDY:    But when I refused to go, you convinced the kids to sit me down in the living room—

GLEN:    I didn't know what else to do.

SANDY:    Like some kind of intervention.

GLEN:    We had the party coming up.

SANDY:    *(What a lame excuse.)* Oh, the party!

GLEN:    You wouldn't go with me to the doctor, I thought you might listen to them.

SANDY:    Well, that sure as hell backfired, didn't it?

GLEN:    Yep.

SANDY:    You pull a stunt like that, you get yourself kicked out.

GLEN:    Apparently. But I keep telling myself it wasn't you who did it.

SANDY:    What?

GLEN:    You're not yourself.

SANDY:    Oh, but I am, though.

GLEN:    We've all been noticing things for a while, but since Christmas, it's gotten worse.

SANDY:    They're called senior moments.

GLEN:    No, honey—

SANDY:    The number of times you've walked into a room and forgotten what you're doing there?

GLEN:    This is not the same thing.

SANDY:    It is.

GLEN:     Then go to the doctor and let him tell you that.

SANDY:    You know, it's pretty rich, you telling me to go see someone.

GLEN:     Okay.

SANDY:    After all these years of me asking you the same thing.

GLEN:     Okay!

SANDY:    Because there is no question there was something wrong with you.

GLEN:     We're not talking about me.

SANDY:    I am. It's a wonder I tolerated you as long as I did.

GLEN:     Yeah? Why did you?

SANDY:    Because I told myself that you'd figure it out. "Maybe he'll relax when he gets older," "When things slow down," "When he retires," but no, it just got worse. And where were the kids then? Not harping on you to get help.

GLEN:     They were, as a matter of fact.

SANDY:    Bullshit.

GLEN:     Greg was.

SANDY:    And you didn't listen. So why should I?

GLEN:     Sandy.

SANDY:    Everybody else, though, they had no idea what you were really like. "Glen? He's just getting old." "He's moody." "Oh Mom, he's always been anxious." For the rest of the world, you put on a pretty good show—learned that from your mother. But with me? Different story.

GLEN:     I told you I'm working on it.

SANDY:     Now.

GLEN:     I'm walking; going to yoga.

SANDY:     It'll take more than downward dog to fix you.

GLEN:     Okay. Can we get back to you, please?

SANDY:     No, we're talking about you, Glen. For years, I've begged you to go talk to someone.

GLEN:     Not years.

SANDY:     Ever since the night we thought you were dying.

GLEN:     Dying?

SANDY:     Our anniversary with the paramedics?

GLEN:     *(It was nothing.)* Oh, that.

SANDY:     That was what? Five, six years ago? And you've done nothing about it.

GLEN:     All right.

SANDY:     The next day, we sat right here and I told you to get help and you didn't.

GLEN:     *(Sound familiar?)* Hello?

SANDY:     I said, "Do it for me," but that wasn't enough.

GLEN:     No, that's not—

SANDY:     *I* wasn't enough. Do you remember that?

GLEN:     …Yeah.

SANDY:          …Yeah.

> *Transition to six years ago, the day after GLEN and SANDY's 44th anniversary. It's a grey evening. We hear the wind in the trees, and some low, distant thunder. A storm is coming in off the lake.*
>
> *GLEN and SANDY have just finished dinner.*

GLEN:           You done?

SANDY:          Yeah.

> *GLEN goes to stand, to clear the table.*

No, no, no, I can do it.

> *She starts clearing the table. He sits back down.*

You barely ate a thing.

GLEN:           Wasn't hungry.

SANDY:          Boys who don't eat their dinner don't get dessert.

GLEN:           (*Looks out.*) We're gonna get that storm.

SANDY:          It might pass us by. (*She gets her cell phone out of her pocket.*) What does the app say?

GLEN:           Forget the app, look at that cloud.

> *But she's looking at her phone.*

Should we head home?

SANDY:          Do you want to?

GLEN:           Well, this roof.

SANDY:    We've got buckets.

GLEN:    I really need to fix that downspout.

*He goes to stand again.*

SANDY:    Glen, sit.

GLEN:    I didn't have a heart attack.

SANDY:    Yeah, thank God. (*She heads inside with the dishes.*)

GLEN:    It was the food at that restaurant. I asked for no hot peppers.

SANDY:    (*From inside.*) It wasn't the food.

GLEN:    Greg and Nicky like that place?

SANDY:    (*Off.*) Yes, they went there for their anniversary.

GLEN:    Anniversary?

SANDY:    (*Returning.*) Of their first date.

GLEN:    They've been together a year? Time flies. The prices on that menu, though!

SANDY:    They gave us a gift certificate. Greg can afford it.

GLEN:    You'd have to be a drug lord to eat there.

SANDY:    Successful entrepreneur.

GLEN:    "The Mr. Christie of Cannabis." Happy forty-four years, Mom and Dad. Here, have some heartburn so bad you think you're dying.

SANDY:    Glen…it wasn't heartburn.

GLEN:    Those paramedics didn't know what they were talking about.

SANDY:    They did. You've been through a lot lately. Your mom? You never let yourself grieve. And now, with Bill being sick, you're under a lot of stress.

GLEN:    I'm fine.

SANDY:    You're not. All that stuff builds up in a person and last night, it…rang the alarm.

GLEN:    I just haven't been sleeping well.

SANDY:    No, Glen, it was a panic attack. Or anxiety, or something.

> *GLEN gets up, dismissing this.*

You're not doing well. You need to take some time off.

GLEN:    Yeah? And who's going to run things?

SANDY:    Tim. The staff.

GLEN:    One of us needs to be there.

SANDY:    The business will survive without one of the Golden brothers overseeing every little detail.

GLEN:    When Bill gets through this round of chemo, we'll see. Maybe I can take a week off then.

SANDY:    No, now. It'll be good practice for when you retire.

GLEN:    Whoa, whoa, whoa.

SANDY:    We're at that age. All our friends are doing it.

GLEN:    Well, not me. Not yet.

SANDY:    See, this is what you do: you bury yourself in work instead of dealing with stuff.

GLEN:        No.

SANDY:       You've always done this. I don't understand why you want to keep working. You never liked selling cars in the first place.

GLEN:        Turns out I'm good at it.

SANDY:       I'm just saying you can stop. You can do something else.

GLEN:        What would I do?

SANDY:       I don't know, golf; drive the girls to soccer; fix the downspout. Anything.

GLEN:        You don't show any signs of slowing down.

SANDY:       No, I am. I think I'm done.

GLEN:        Yeah, right.

SANDY:       I worked so hard on this latest book and it's a giant flop.

GLEN:        It was just released.

SANDY:       The sales aren't there. I convinced them to publish it—my big serious novel, the one I always wanted to write—and whaddaya know? No one wants to read it.

GLEN:        I read it.

SANDY:       Yeah, and you hated it.

GLEN:        I didn't *hate* it. It was just…different.

SANDY:       That was the point.

GLEN:        I wanted the couple to end up together at the end.

SANDY:    But I already wrote that story—nineteen times. I don't know. I think I'm going to pack it in.

          *She starts to head inside. GLEN is looking out.*

GLEN:     The wind's picking up.

SANDY:    *(Turning back, at the door.)* Do you want to go to Alaska?

GLEN:     What?

SANDY:    *(Returning to him.)* The Dempseys went, on a cruise. We could do that.

GLEN:     An Alaskan cruise?

SANDY:    Murray loved it. Patty told me all about it, down on the beach. They saw whales. You'd like that.

GLEN:     Whales?

SANDY:    Killer whales. Remember that movie? You loved that.

GLEN:     What movie?

SANDY:    The one with the whale. We had it on VHS. Greg made us watch it.

GLEN:     *ET?*

SANDY:    No! It had a whale.

GLEN:     I have no idea what you're talking about.

SANDY:    Forget it. We don't have to go to Alaska, we can go anywhere you like.

GLEN:     I want to go home. I want to go back to work. I had one bad night.

SANDY:          If you won't take time off, at least go talk to someone.

GLEN:           I'm talking to you, aren't I?

SANDY:          A professional.

GLEN:           No, thank you.

SANDY:          Greg sees someone; he really likes her.

GLEN:           I'm not bipolar.

SANDY:          No, I don't think you are. But you're something. Your mom never got the help she needed—

GLEN:           My mom was a different story.

SANDY:          Don't tell me that, tell a therapist.

GLEN:           You want me to tell Greg's shrink all about my terrible, awful childhood?

SANDY:          If it would help. Or tell them what was going through your head last night.

GLEN:           *(The shrink.)* "So, Mr. Golden, what seems to be your trouble?" *(Himself.)* "Well, doc, I thought I was having the big one, so my wife called 911, but it turns out I either shouldn't have had the fish tacos or I am, what you might call in your profession, cuckoo for cocoa puffs."

SANDY:          It's a start.

                *Beat. GLEN sits on the steps of the deck.*

GLEN:           You know what came into my head last night? When we were waiting for the ambulance?

SANDY:          What?

GLEN:        Something that happened on our first date.

SANDY:       What, when you slipped that carny forty bucks to let you win the stuffed poodle?

GLEN:        That was our second date. And it was sixty bucks. No, when we went to that play.

SANDY:       *(Joining him, sitting.)* Oh. What made you think of that?

GLEN:        I don't know, it just came into my head.

SANDY:       Do you remember what play it was?

GLEN:        Shakespeare.

SANDY:       Uh huh?

GLEN:        There were witches.

SANDY:       And it was called…?

GLEN:        That's not the point. The point is, there I was, the guy who sold your dad a car—

SANDY:       Tried to sell him a car.

GLEN:        It's my memory; may I continue?

                    *SANDY relents.*

             Tried to sell him a car. I might not have closed the deal, but you came with him for the test drive, and I got your number, so…worked out.

SANDY:       The play was a test, you know.

GLEN:        What?

SANDY:       My parents couldn't use their tickets, so I thought, "All right, let's see if this car salesman is really interested."

GLEN:   Well, I was. But I had no idea a fancy Shakespeare play would have so much blood. Right from the word "go," they all come in, covered in it, and I closed my eyes, but then I thought, "No, she'll see, she'll think you're sleeping." So I tried just looking to the side, but a guy comes right up the aisle, like, "O my good Lord, they doth cut off my arm."

SANDY:   One of Shakespeare's most beautiful lines.

GLEN:   I remember she was good, the wife. But it was the moment when the main guy comes back in, just dripping in blood, like, "Oh jeez, I killed him," that I thought I was gonna pass out.

SANDY:   I know. I was sitting right there.

GLEN:   And do you remember what you did?

SANDY:   Yeah, I thought, "What is this guy's deal?"

GLEN:   You held my hand.

SANDY:   Did I?

GLEN:   Yeah, and I felt…I don't know…better. I guess that's why I thought of it, last night. Cuz there we were, thinking I was a goner, and you, you took hold of my hand, and I… I remembered that. All those years ago.

SANDY:   Well, whatever you're going through now…I can't just hold your hand and make it go away. Go talk to someone. Please? Do it for me.

*The rain starts.*

GLEN:   Ah! Here it comes.

> *SANDY gets up and takes out her phone, looking at the app.*

SANDY:   Oh, God. It's heading straight for us. (*Heading inside.*) Where are the buckets?

GLEN:   Under the sink.

> *She gets to the door, but he stays sitting, looking out. She turns back.*

SANDY:   You coming in?

GLEN:   In a sec.

> *SANDY goes in, leaving GLEN alone.*

I'm fine.

> **Transition back to the present.** *The sun has nearly set now.*
>
> *GLEN stands—it's difficult and painful with his back. SANDY comes outside.*

SANDY:   *Free Willy.*

GLEN:   What?

SANDY:   The movie with the whale. It's called *Free Willy.*

GLEN:   That sounds like a porno.

SANDY:   Do you think the girls would like to see that?

GLEN:   They're probably too old for it now.

SANDY:   No. Do we still have the tape?

GLEN:   Probably, but we don't have a VCR.

SANDY:   (*Looking out.*) Did it clear up?

GLEN:   Hm?

SANDY:       I thought it was going to rain.

GLEN:        No, it rained earlier.

SANDY:       Oh. Bill and Raquel have a VCR, don't they? We can borrow theirs.

GLEN:        What?

SANDY:       Bill tapes all the baseball games. He's never figured out his PVR. I'll call and ask him.

*She reaches in her pocket for her phone.*

GLEN:        Sandy.

SANDY:       Where's my phone?

GLEN:        You can't call Bill.

SANDY:       Oh, was today chemo?

GLEN:        No…

SANDY:       I'll talk to Raquel, then—

GLEN:        Honey.

SANDY:       Or I'll text her. Where the hell is my phone? I just had it.

GLEN:        It's okay.

SANDY:       (*Looking for it.*) It was in my hand!

GLEN:        All right, we'll find it.

SANDY:       I swear to God, everything has legs. Gets up and walks away.

GLEN:        Why don't we call Raquel later?

SANDY:       Where is it?

GLEN:        Here, do you want to use mine?

SANDY:        No!

GLEN:         Sandy, take a breath.

SANDY:        Where the hell did I put it?

GLEN:         Did you leave it inside? When you got changed?

SANDY:        What?

GLEN:         You want me to check?

SANDY:        Yes! Help me look!

GLEN:         Okay, I'll look inside, okay?

> *He goes in. She has picked up her purse. She searches through it frantically.*

SANDY:        Stupid, goddamn, fucking purse! Where is it!?

> *With this, she dumps the contents of her purse on the table. Beat. She stops.*
>
> *GLEN comes back with her cell phone.*

GLEN:         It was on the dresser.

SANDY:        ...Bill's dead.

GLEN:         Yeah.

SANDY:        He died.

GLEN:         Five years ago.

SANDY:        Oh my God.

GLEN:         It's okay.

SANDY:        Bill's gone.

GLEN:         Yeah.

SANDY:   I think I, uh… I think I got a little mixed up. Cuz we were talking about when he was sick and I— I thought he was still… Oh, God.

*She breaks down. GLEN holds her.*

GLEN:   It's okay. You're okay. Shhh. I'm here. I'm right here. I got you.

*Beat. The embrace ends.*

We've gotta get you checked out.

SANDY:   No.

GLEN:   They can tell us what's going on.

SANDY:   I don't want to know.

GLEN:   Oh, honey. I think we already do. You watched me do this for years: deny, ignore, repeat. You said it yourself: it won't work. I'll go talk to someone, okay? Tomorrow morning, I'll make myself an appointment. I'll do that if you agree to do the tests. Okay?

*SANDY's phone gets a text alert. GLEN's still got it.*

Oh. *(He looks.)* Your publisher.

*She shakes her head; she can't deal with it.*

*(Reading the text message.)* "Don't worry about dinner. Let's chat soon about this new book."

SANDY:   …I can't write a book.

GLEN:   You don't have to. You did that. You wrote lots.

SANDY:   And they were all a big, fat lie.

GLEN:   What?

SANDY:      Except one, they all ended happily ever after—when everyone's young and in love.

GLEN:       That's not a lie.

SANDY:      It's not the whole truth. A lot of shit happens after that.

GLEN:       Honey—

SANDY:      You want your happy ending, Glen? Go be with Patty Dempsey.

GLEN:       I don't want Patty Dempsey.

SANDY:      If her mind goes, she'll just get a new one.

GLEN:       I want you.

SANDY:      But you're a mess. You can't take care of me.

GLEN:       I'll sort myself out.

SANDY:      Greg checks on me, I don't need you there.

GLEN:       You do.

SANDY:      We drive each other around the bend.

GLEN:       Too bad! I love you.

SANDY:      Yeah? Well, love can't fix this. Don't you see? If I go to the doctor, then we know. We know for sure, and we know how that goes. And I don't want to put you through that.

GLEN:       It's what I signed up for.

SANDY:      No one signs up for this. I can remember the tiniest detail from fifty years ago, clear as day, but ask me what happened ten minutes ago? (*A gesture for "nothing."*) And what happens when it gets worse? When I can't remember our life together? Can't remember us? Can't remember you?

GLEN:  Just cuz you can't remember something doesn't mean it didn't happen; doesn't mean it didn't matter. What matters is: we did it. Everything gets forgotten, sooner or later. But we are not there yet. We are not done.

> *Pause. SANDY looks out. The sun has set completely.*

SANDY:  It got dark.

GLEN:  Yeah. Do you want to go home? I can drive you. I don't have to stay.

SANDY:  No. We'll go home tomorrow. We'll deal with this tomorrow.

> *GLEN goes to sit, but his back twinges with pain.*

GLEN:  Ah.

SANDY:  When did you get so old?

GLEN:  I don't know. I can't remember.

> *Beat. SANDY looks out.*

SANDY:  I like it here. Look! You can see the stars!

> *Music—an instrumental part of their first dance song that GLEN sang.*

> *SANDY looks at the stars, as she did on their wedding night. She reaches out and takes GLEN's hand.*

> *As the lights fade, the Goldens hold hands and look out to the universe…*

> *End of play.*